TOOLS FOR CAREGIVERS

- **F&P LEVEL:** E
- **WORD COUNT:** 47
- **CURRICULUM CONNECTIONS:** animals, habitats, nature

Skills to Teach

- **HIGH-FREQUENCY WORDS:** a, an, are, at, big, come, goes, has, is, it, its, out, small, the, to, will
- **CONTENT WORDS:** burrow, claws, day, during, ears, eats, fruit, hears, mice, mouse, night, owl, runs, safe, sleeps, tail, whiskers
- **PUNCTUATION:** exclamation point, periods
- **WORD STUDY:** long a, spelled ai (tail); long e, spelled ea (ears, eats, hears); long e, spelled ee (sleeps); long o, spelled ow (burrow); ow sound, spelled ou (mouse, out); ow sound, spelled ow (owl); oo sound, spelled ui (fruit)
- **TEXT TYPE:** information report

Before Reading Activities

- Read the title and give a simple statement of the main idea.
- Have students "walk" though the book and talk about what they see in the pictures.
- Introduce new vocabulary by having students predict the first letter and locate the word in the text.
- Discuss any unfamiliar concepts that are in the text.

After Reading Activities

Explain that a mouse is very small. It cannot defend itself from predators, like the owl in the book. One way it stays safe is in its burrow. Explain that burrows are tunnels or holes in the ground. Can readers think of any other animals that live in burrows? What other animal homes can readers think of, such as trees, nests, hives, or dens? What animals live in these?

Tadpole Books are published by Jump!, 5357 Penn Avenue South, Minneapolis, MN 55419, www.jumplibrary.com

Copyright ©2020 Jump. International copyright reserved in all countries. No part of this book may be reproduced in any form without written permission from the publisher.

Editor: Jenna Trnka **Designer:** Michelle Sonnek

Photo Credits: Eric Isselee/Shutterstock, cover, 1, 8–9; Charles Bergman/Shutterstock, 2mr; Alan Tunnicliffe/Shutterstock, 3; Tsekhmister/Shutterstock, 2bl, 2br, 4–5; Rudmer Zwerver/Shutterstock, 2tr, 2ml, 6–7; Joe McDonald/Shutterstock, 10–11; LazyFocus/Shutterstock, 2tl, 12–13; Jeff Lepore/Alamy, 14–15; Paul Tymon/Shutterstock, 16.

Library of Congress Cataloging-in-Publication Data
Names: Nilsen, Genevieve, author.
Title: Mice / by Genevieve Nilsen.
Description: Tadpole edition. | Minneapolis, MN: Jump!, Inc., (2020) | Series: Backyard animals | Audience: Age 3–6. | Includes index.
Identifiers: LCCN 2019016663 (print) | LCCN 2019018519 (ebook) | ISBN 9781645271017 (ebook) | ISBN 9781645270997 (hardcover: alk. paper) | ISBN 9781645271000 (paperback)
Subjects: LCSH: Mice—Juvenile literature.
Classification: LCC QL737.R6 (ebook) | LCC QL737.R6 N55 2020 (print) | DDC 599.35/3—dc23
LC record available at https://lccn.loc.gov/2019016663

ANIMALS

CE

by Genevieve Nilsen

TABLE OF CONTENTS

tadpole
books

WORDS TO KNOW

burrow

claws

fruit

owl

tail

whiskers

MICE

Mice are small.

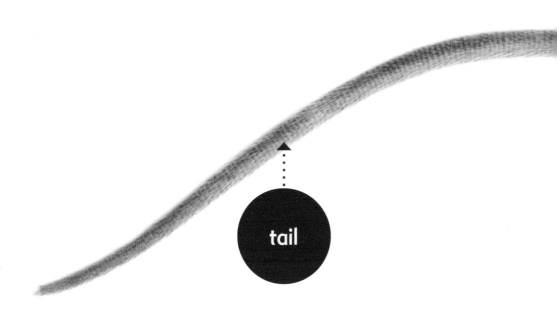

tail

A mouse has a tail.

whiskers ·····▶

It has whiskers.

It has claws.

claw

It eats fruit.

ear

It has big ears.

It hears an owl.

It runs!

It goes to its burrow.

burrow

It is safe.

It sleeps during the day.

It will come out at night.

LET'S REVIEW!

This mouse is eating seeds. What is it using to hold and eat its food?

INDEX